J⊙B
SEARCH

TEEN
INTERVIEW TIPS AND STRATEGIES TO
GET HIRED

PATRICIA DORCH

Limit of Liability/Disclaimer of Warranty. The author and publisher have used their best efforts in preparing this book. This publication contains the opinions, ideas and recommendations of its author and publisher. Neither author nor publisher shall be liable for any loss of profit, or risk, personal, including but not limited to special, incidental, consequential, professional or any other commercial or other damages which is incurred as a consequence, directly or indirectly, of the use and application of any of the contents of this book. The accuracy and completeness of the information provided herein and the opinions of stated herein are not guaranteed or warranted to produce any particular results. The advice and strategies contained herein may not be suitable for every individual, organization or situation.

Dorch, Patricia

Job Search: Teen Interview Tips and Strategies to Get Hired / Patricia Dorch

Copyright © **2012 by Patricia Dorch, All Rights Reserved**.

Bulk Purchases: Minimum Order – 50 Books
For information about special discounts for bulk purchases please contact
Patricia Dorch at:

Website: www.jobsearchteensbook.com
Email: PatriciaDorch@jobsearchteensbook.com

Email: Patricia@execudress.com
Website: www.execudress.com

Printed in the United States of America

ISBN-13: 978-0-9816854-5-8

ISBN-10: 0-9816854-5-5

DEDICATION

This book is dedicated to Willie Mae Dorch,
Francine Dorch
and
In Memory of Norman Dorch

ACKNOWLEDGEMENT

I want to extend my personal and sincere thanks to all who have dedicated their time, expertise and advice for this book. Your knowledge and support have contributed to my success.

CONTENTS

"Empowered To Get Hired"
-PATRICIA DORCH

Job Search
Teen Interview Tips and Strategies to Get Hired

INTRODUCTION

What skills do employer's look for in a new employee?

Today employers look for employees who demonstrate professionalism in the workplace. The basic requirements to get hired include good interview skills; wear business clothing appropriate for an interview and work, have good character, excellent listening, and oral and written communication skills, interpersonal communication skills, public speaking, problem solving, leadership, business and dining etiquette and other skills are required to get hired and promoted.

These essential skills will help you accomplish the mission and goals of the organization and be successful in your career. To get a job you will compete for employment with your peers, college graduates, experienced workers, professionals and retirees. Without these important skills it will be difficult to get hired and perform your job to maintain employment.

Why do employers prefer experienced workers?

Employers prefer experienced workers because it reduces hiring, training and turnover costs associated with new employees. Employees who have valuable skills can start work with little or no training.

How can I learn skills I need to land a good job?

You can develop important skills by participating in an internship, volunteering, working on a project, leading others in a mentoring group, take a class and read topics that will benefit you at work.

Job Search: Teen Interview Tips and Strategies to Get Hired provide cutting-edge job search and professional skills you can use to market your skills.

Chapter One
How to Make a Great First Impression

Introduction

Do you make a positive first impression?

It takes only a few seconds for someone to form an impression of you based on appearance, *body language, communication skills and your mannerisms.* Each time you meet someone you make a first impression and set the expectations for future relationships. Listed are secrets you can use to make your first impression successful.

Five Secrets for a First Impression

Secret 1: Physical Appearance

- The secret to a great first impression is to present yourself professionally.

- Create a positive impression to set the stage for what others can expect from you in the future.

- Wear clothing that is appropriate for the situation whether it is for work, school, important meetings or another occasion. If you do not know if you should dress business, business casual or casual ask the person in charge.

- Do not feel embarrassed about asking what you should wear. The best way to avoid embarrassment is to arrive for the occasion dressed properly.

Secret 2: Be On Time

- To make a positive first impression plan to arrive 15-20 minutes early for an interview, work, and school and to meet with friends.

- When you make a presentation to a group allow at least one hour set up time for your presentation.

- There is no such thing as a "good excuse" for being late. Arriving early will save you embarrassment and the right step in making a positive first impression.

- Being on time gives you time to relax, socialize with others and focus on the purpose of your meeting.

Secret 3: Be Yourself

* Relax so others in your company will be at ease. Be calm, confident and in control. Your interpersonal skills will determine your relationship with others.

Secret 4: Be Confident

* Positive language will communicate you are confident and have self-assurance.

* Make direct eye contact and greet others with a firm handshake.

Secret 5: Smile

* There is nothing like a smile to make a great first impression. A sincere smile will put you and others at ease.

The Proper Handshake

Why do people shake hands?

The purpose of a handshake is to establish rapport and positive chemistry between two people. A handshake is a form of non-verbal communication. It is appropriate to shake hands at an interview, in business or other social occasions.

Your handshake communicates:

- Professionalism
- Confidence

When to Stand

When should I stand?

It is proper to stand when shaking hands during introductions unless you are seated in an environment such as a restaurant that makes standing difficult. Standing balances the power between you and your contact. The person who is standing is presumed to have the power.

A firm handshake communicates:

- Self-Assurance
- Self-Confidence
- Interest
- Respect

The Name Game

Has your name ever been mispronounced or spelled incorrectly?

Everyone likes to have his or her name remembered, pronounced, and spelled correctly. Making an effort to remember names strengthens personal and business relationships.

Six simple ways to help you remember names:

1. Listen carefully to people's names.

2. If you are not sure you heard the person's name correctly, or if you did not understand what the person said, ask them to repeat the name.

3. Repeat the name back to the person for reinforcement and confirmation only if you did not understand.

4. Break the name down into syllables for yourself.

5. Connect the name with something familiar to you.

6. Identify something unique about the person and their name.

Appearances Do Count!

Ask yourself, "What image do I project?"

What you wear today could impact your career tomorrow. Dressing appropriately for business is an essential element of doing business and being successful. Never underestimate the power of first impressions. Position yourself where you want to go in your career; your clothing sends a message about how serious you are. Appearances Do Count!

Appearance is based on the following percentages and characteristics:

- Appearance and body language – 55%
- Vocal tone, pacing, and voice inflection – 38%
- Verbal message – 7%

Career opportunities:

- You never know who is observing your appearance.
- Position your appearance for promotions.

- Think about the perception others might have of your non-verbal communication.

- Consider the positive or negative impact your appearance can have on your career and future.

- Make smart decisions.

Twelve Tips for Career Success

Introduction

Have you wondered why other people are happy? Learn the tips they use to be happy.

A positive attitude can help you achieve your career and personal goals, make a situation easier and enjoyable. A positive attitude is essential for success.

When you start a new job, do your homework, work on a project individually or with others, volunteer in your community, meet with friends or family, everything you do should start with a positive attitude. How you begin your encounters with others sets the tone for a positive outcome. A positive attitude will help eliminate negative thoughts of "I can't", I don't want to", "I will not" and others.

Sometimes it's not always possible to maintain a positive attitude. In life things can and will go wrong, when they do use these tips to help you maintain your focus.

Twelve Tips for Career Success

Tip 1: Start your Day Early

- Wake up early so you can plan and prepare for your day without feeling rushed.

Tip 2: Exercise

- Exercise can improve your physical, mental health, and overall positive mood.

Tip 3: Read Inspirational Books

- Inspirational books will encourage you, inspire you, teach you "how to" and help you maintain a positive attitude.

Tip 4: Listen to Motivational CD's or Music

- Listen to motivational CD's or music during your commute or free time will encourage and relax you.

Tip 5: Plan your Week and Day

- Make a daily and weekly plan.

- Set your priorities.

- Focus on things you want and need to accomplish.

Tip 6: Expect the Unexpected

- Understand things will not always go as planned.

- You will learn new skills when you learn how to manage the unexpected experience.

- Adapt to the unexpected situation then re-focus on your plan.

Tip 7: Be Thankful

- Make a list of the things you are thankful for.

- Think about other people who do not have what you have – food, shelter, family, friends and good health.

- Be thankful for someone who loves you and cares about your well being.

Tip 8: Positive People

- Surround yourself with people who are positive and supportive.

- You are judged by the friends with whom you surround yourself.

- Avoid contact with people who are negative or encourage them to consider changing their attitude.

Tip 9: Be Proactive

- Be proactive and take control of your future.

- Set short and long-term goals for yourself.

Tip 10: Humor

- Have a sense of humor, be upbeat and positive.

- Laughing makes you feel good.

Tip 11: New Opportunities

- Successful people embrace new opportunities to learn new skills.

Tip 12: Self Management

- Self management requires you to be responsible and accountable for yourself, behavior and career.

Chapter Three
Interpersonal Communication Skills

Interpersonal communication skills improve self confidence, self-esteem, work and personal relationships. These skills are essential to get hired, promoted and have a successful career. Effective communication improves writing, conversation, body language, public speaking and other skills.

Better Business Writing for Successful Communication

Do you send a cover letter with your resume when you apply for jobs?

Today's business world is information driven and good writing skills will increase your chances of achieving employment and promotional opportunities at work. Most employers require a cover letter with your application. The purpose of the cover letter is to focus on applicants who can communicate their skills in writing. In the workplace good communication is vital to good business relationships and reduces misunderstandings.

The ability to effectively communicate your thoughts in writing will enhance your career success. Listed are tips to learn to write well.

Eight Tips for Successful Communication

1. Keep it Simple

- Make your point immediately – say what you have to say.

- Use words sparingly.

- Avoid long sentences.

- Ask if you do not understand.

2. Avoid Jargon

- Use language that all cultures can understand.

3. Write Once, Check Three Times

- Proofread after you write – do not rely on spell and grammar check.

- Allow time to proofread by setting your document aside to review.

- Our brain is tricky – we tend to read what we want to be there instead of what is written.

- Walk away for a few minutes and then re-read it out loud.

4. Check Your Tone

- When you read your message out loud – it helps you hear your tone.

- Make sure you say what you want it to say and how you want it communicated.

5. Names, Genders and Title

- If you are not positive of a spelling of persons name, gender or title confirm with someone who knows them before you write your document.

- Address people by their formal name until you know if they prefer a nickname.

- A signature on a document gives you permission to address a person by the name signed.

- Do not take it upon yourself to call someone by a nickname you have chosen for them.

6. Be Professional

- Informal communication does not mean unprofessional.

- Do not use jokes – it might be misinterpreted.

- Do not talk about others.

- Be aware – your email may be forwarded to others.

- Most businesses keep copies of all written communication.

7. Remember – Who? What? When? Where? Why? and How?

- **Who** is the audience that will receive the memo?
- **What** should they know?
- **When** and **where** will it apply?
- **Why** it is important?
- **How** should they use the information you provided?

8. Call to Action

- **What** is the reader expected to do?
- **When** should they do it?
- **When** do you expect a response?

"Formal communication in the workplace shows your professionalism."

-PATRICIA DORCH

Teen Speak

Use the Right Words at Work

Do you use teen speak to communicate at work as you do with family and friends? Do you use slang, acronyms and abbreviations to take short cuts to communicate? Did you take a short cut on your job application, cover letter, e-mail or thank you letter?

Teen Speak is a popular *informal* accepted communication method used among teens and young adults in the *social* world. It's important to know when and where to use informal communication. Most people have two vocabularies one for work and a less formal communication for family and friends.

In the workplace communication is always *formal* and *professional* in verbal, e-mail and text communication with management and co-workers. At work be accountable and responsible for speaking and writing standards. Be mindful of words and abbreviations such as **yeah, huh, 4, uh, whatever, like, cause, U2, hey** and others that should *not* be used in formal communication. In a professional environment teen speak is inappropriate, hurts your credibility and puts your career at risk. How you communicate impacts your ability to get hired, promoted and compete with national and international employees.

The Power of Positive Body Language

Introduction

What does your body language say to others about you?

Body language is a non-verbal form of communication by which your expressions, gestures, and movements convey unspoken messages to those around you. Workplace body language can change how others perceive you and is crucial to your career success.

Non-verbal body language may differ depending on what culture you are speaking to. When working with people of different cultures it might be useful for you to understand non-verbal body language from multiple cultures.

Listed are tools for positive and less effective body language and how to best use or avoid them.

Nine Positive Body Language Tools

1. **Eye Contact** – Make positive direct eye contact with others.

2. **Head** – Hold your head up straight.

3. **Posture** – Stand or sit tall with your shoulders back. Exude charisma, competence and confidence in your posture.

4. **Hands** – Use purposeful hand gestures.

5. **Attitude** – Your attitude starts on the inside and shows on the outside.

6. **Personal Space** – Allow 15-20 inches of personal space between you and others.

7. **Walk** – Walk with confidence, ease and grace.

8. **Body Movement** – Move your body confidently and gracefully.

9. **Smile** – Have an engaging smile and light up the room.

Eight Body Language Tips to Avoid

1. **Eyes** – Rolling your eyes at others.

2. **Clenching Fists** – Communicates you are experiencing tension, anxiety or possible aggressive behavior.

3. **Arms** – Arms crossed over your chest can be view as defensive.

4. **Neck Movements** – Shows lack of controlled behavior and inappropriate in the workplace and other situations.

5. **Finger Snapping, Pointing and Arm Movements** – Unprofessional and inappropriate.

6. **Hands on Hips** – This can translate – "I'm not in agreement with what you are saying."

7. **Touching Others** – Touching others although

the intention may be friendly could be misinterpreted. If you touch another person observe their reaction to see how your contact affects them. You may consider asking them how they feel when you touch them or perhaps not touch at all.

8. **Barriers** – Standing behind a chair, or podium, crossing your arms over your chest or speaking to someone behind a computer creates a barrier to communication.

Although you may think others do not notice your body language it does not go unnoticed. Be conscious of non-verbal body language and how it can communicate positive or negative messages. Focus on *positive gestures* that will enhance your personality and help you be successful.

"Small conversations are an effective way to learn about each other."

-PATRICIA DORCH

How to Develop Good Conversation Skills

Introduction

Good conversation skills are important in every aspect of your career. The ability to be comfortable and hold conversations with people of different cultural backgrounds will position you for a successful career.

Do not allow a persons position or title prevent you from holding a business or cordial conversation. Every good conversation consists of three key elements to be successful. First, be a good listener, second, do not interrupt the speaker, three, wait until the speaker asks for feedback or gives you a cue to participate.

How do you begin a conversation with people you do not know?

A conversation can begin with a topic you have in common, and then direct the conversation in the direction you want to go. Conversations about the weather, current events, holiday events or a hobby are general topics.

At work be careful not to be critical of company policies and procedures or co-workers during your conversation. Learn the secrets that will improve your conversations with others.

Five Conversation Secrets for Success

Secret 1: Focus

- Focus on the speaker.
- Observe the speaker verbal and non-verbal body language.

Secret 2: Show Emotion

- Nodding your head.
- Lean forward.
- Timely interjections.

Secret 3: Give and Take Conversations

- Do not control the entire conversation.
- Do not speak longer than 3 minutes.

- Allow others to participate in your conversation.
- Do not interrupt an existing conversation.
- Do not change the conversation of the group you have just joined.

Secret 4: Criticism

- Do not criticize others in public or private.

- Offer your opinion without criticizing their point of view.

- Ask questions that might help you better understand their perspective.

Secret 5: Sex, Religion and Politics

- Do not discuss or participate in "hot button" topics such as sex, religion or politics.

- Keep personal views to yourself – your opinions can make or break your career.

- When in the company of those who are discussing these topics practice good listening skills.

- When asked for your opinion – state "I have no opinion at this time." This would be a good time to excuse yourself and move to another conversation.

Engage Your Connection

What tips can I use to engage a person or group of people in a conversation?

The letters in the word "engage" will help you remember the process of engaging your connection in a conversation.

Eye – Establish and maintain good eye contact.

Nod – Nod to encourage communication.

Greet – Greet people with a friendly smile, hello, and handshake.

Attention – Focus your attention on what is being said.

Gesturing – Gesturing your hands when you talk enhances your message.

Ease – Be at ease and comfortable with your connection.

Fourteen Rules for Active Listening

What is active listening?

Active listening is a listening skill. It is twice as hard as talking because it takes practice to acquire good listening skills. Information is sent by a speaker and received by an active listener. By moving your face and keeping your eyes on the speaker you can easily adapt good listening skills.

An open mind and focus will help you concentrate on the message and receive information. Active listening is an important life skill. Listed are rules to strengthen active listening skills.

Fourteen Rules for Active Listening

Rule 1: Understand

- Listen to understand the speaker.

Rule 2: Read Between the Lines

- Read between the lines – listen for what is *not* said.

Rule 3: Do not Interrupt

- Do not interrupt the speaker.

Rule 4: Participate

- Listen for cues to participate in the conversation.

Rule 5: Look

- Look at the person who is speaking.

Rule 6: Eye Contact

- Establish eye contact with the speaker.

Rule 7: Body Language

- Good listeners lead with their facial expression and body language.

Rule 8: Concentrate

- Concentrate on the message.

Rule 9: Distractions

* Eliminate external distractions.

Rule 10: Write

* Write down notes or questions you may need to ask.

Rule 11: Evaluate

* Evaluate the message delivered.

Rule 12: Conclusions

* Do not jump to conclusions.

Rule 13: Listen

* Do not stop listening.

Rule 14: Verbal and Non-verbal Cues

* Be alert to verbal and non-verbal cues by the speaker.

Public Speaking for Career Success

Introduction

Public speaking skills are essential to effectively compete for employment or seek a promotion. Use public speaking skills to sell yourself at a job interview or at work will enable you to confidently communicate your ideas and thoughts to management, peers, clients and customers.

Are you comfortable speaking to a group of people?

Today there are really are no situations where you are not using public speaking skills to communicate. The benefits of public speaking skills include a new job, promotion and improved relationships. What should I do to improve my public speaking skills? Listed are simple steps to help you speak for success.

Seven Simple Steps to Speak Easy

1. *Join* a youth leadership program or organization at school or in your community that teaches public speaking skills.

2. *Plan* and *organize* your presentation before you present to an audience.

3. Always *practice out loud* several times before you present anything important to a group or individual. Practice increases your confidence and improves your speaking and presentation skills.

4. Ask for *feedback* from your teacher, management, a family member, friend and someone you trust such as a mentor.

5. *Volunteer* to present to small groups 1-5 people to build confidence and comfort.

6. *Do your homework.* You are the expert on the topic you are presenting. Be prepared to answer questions and over come objections to your ideas.

7. *Public speaking* improves your skills and positions you for career success.

Summary

Interpersonal communication skills are important to accomplish the goals and objectives of your employer. Written communication should be clearly written. Verbal communication should be clearly stated. Good interpersonal skills allow you to build relationships, understand people better, work well in a team environment and develop skills you need to be successful in your career. When you achieve good interpersonal skills you will see the rewards at work and in your personal life.

Employers hire employees who have character traits that distinguish them from other candidates. These employees are accountable, responsible, and productive and have a track record of achievements.

How can you stand out from other candidates looking for work?

Top candidates are in demand by employers – they want employees who can add value to their organization. Listed are ten character traits of valuable employees.

1. Listen to Instructions

- Pay attention to what you are told to do.

- Listen carefully and do not jump to the wrong conclusions.

- Ask questions to confirm you understand instructions.

- Patience prevents you from rushing to judgment.

- Active listening reduces mistakes and prevents accidents.

2. Be Responsible

- Know your job description.

- Pay attention to detail.

- Know what to do and when to do it.

- Be aware of your co-workers responsibilities.

- Be aware how your responsibilities affect others work.

- When things go wrong take responsibility for your actions.

3. Take Initiative

- Show initiative – do not wait to be told what to do.

- A self motivated employee gets things done.

- Help others when it is clear they need help.

- Look for ways to solve problems.

4. Compliment Others

- Make it a practice to give credit to others.

- Share the spotlight with others when you are complimented for a job well done.

- Team workers will respect you for sharing the spotlight with them.

5. Be Courteous

- Know how to interact with others.

- Acknowledge a compliment by saying "thank you."

- When someone tells you "thank you" say "you're welcome."

- Politely acknowledge someone who speaks to you – do not ignore them.

- Be kind and show respect to others.

6. Be Positive

- When things go wrong – do not complain.

- A problem needs a solution.

- Be seen as a problem solver.

7. Be Dependable

· Do not make it a habit of being late or sick.

· Show people they can depend on you to keep your commitments.

· Arrive to work early or on time.

· Honor all commitments.

· Perform tasks well and on time.

· Strive for excellence and quality.

· Build a positive reputation that will follow you.

8. Be Healthy

· Get plenty of rest and eat healthy foods.

· Exercise makes you feel better.

· If you are sick do not go to work until you feel better.

· Do not wait until the last minute to inform your employer you will not be at work.

9. Self-Discipline

- Manage your time.

- Stay focused.

- Avoid distractions outside of your job.

10. Expectations

- Do more than you are expected to do.

- Take on assignments others do not want to do.

- Be visible and valuable.

These character traits will make you more marketable and give you the advantage over other candidates. Character traits are instrumental in being hired, leading others and being seen as a valuable asset to an employer.

"Listen to understand from the speaker's perspective."

-PATRICIA DORCH

Chapter Five
Fifteen Keys to Conflict Resolution

Have you had a disagreement with a teacher, coach, manager, supervisor, or one of your peers? How do you resolve conflict?

As you develop relationships with others you will encounter conflict. Learn life skills to resolve conflict without getting emotional and taking the conflict personally. Conflict resolution skills will build confidence, self esteem and teach you how to effectively manage uncomfortable situations. These skills will teach you how to respectfully disagree and show your professionalism. Listed are keys to manage and resolve conflicts.

Five Keys to Anger Management

1. **Calm down.** Calming down will help you see the problem more clearly and determine a strategy to manage the issue.

2. **Anger vs. Issue.** Separate your anger from the issue. Focus on the issue to help you manage anger.

3. **Give it time.** Calm down before you discuss a problem.

4. **Old conflicts.** Let go of the past by not bringing it up.

5. **Ask an adult for help.** If you can not solve your conflict ask an adult for help.

Five Keys to Communication Conflict

1. **Talk directly to the person** – Speaking directly to the person will increase confidence and avoid miscommunication by others who speak for you.

2. **Get the facts.** Gather the facts and understand the other person perspective before you jump to conclusions.

3. **Listen.** Actively listen to understand the speaker. Only one person should speak at a time without interruption by the other person.

4. **Use "I" statements.** Use "I" statements rather than "You" statements. The use of "You"

statements may make the other person feel threatened and not open to listening to what you have to say.

5. **Apologize.** Apologize and take responsibility for your actions when you have done something wrong or you have hurt someone. The other person will have more respect for you as a result of your apology.

Five Keys to Social Conflict

1. **Be respectful.** Be respectful and separate the conflict from the person. When the conflict is resolved you will have maintained your relationship.

2. **Do not involve others.** Keep the conflict only between the parties that are involved. Do not involve others who will tend to support their friend.

3. **Reflective listening.** Reflective listening skills will help you determine if you understood the person correctly by repeating back to them your understanding what was said for clarification.

4. **Do Not Take Things Seriously.** Sometimes the best way to resolve conflict is to laugh about it and start over.

5. **Compromise.** Not every battle is meant to be won by you. Be open and willing to compromise – use a give and take strategy that is acceptable to both parties.

Use communication skills to resolve conflict at work, school, at home and other situations where you have disagreements. Conflict resolution skills require you to be a good listener, respectful of others, brain storm solutions to solve problems, reach a compromise and value relationships of people.

Sixteen Core Principles of Leadership
Communication

Introduction

Do you have leadership skills?

Leadership skills are essential in a competitive and global marketplace. In a multicultural workplace, cultural and social sensitivity is essential to building relationships with all people of different cultures, nationalities, religious beliefs and professional backgrounds. In our growing and diverse marketplace effective leadership communication extends beyond your "comfort zone" – people who look, talk or act like you.

How can I learn the secrets of leadership communication?

In addition to work, internships or volunteer work you can learn leadership skills by joining a school student leadership program or youth leadership organization in your community. Listed are core principles of leadership communication.

Sixteen Core Principles of Leadership Communication

1. *Positive* attitude.

2. *Think we, not I.* Accomplish goals for group success not for personal gain.

3. *Connect* with the person or audience.

4. Establishes *trust* and *respect* of those you lead.

5. Builds *morale* and manages conflict.

6. *Listen* to understand the person or audience.

7. *Be generous* with your time and concern for employees and customers.

8. *Inspire* employees to work hard.

9. *Encourage* people to *work together* and accept differences.

10. *Manages* body language and emotional control.

11. *Confident* communication style.

12. Engages people so they are relaxed.

13. Public speaking and *presentation skills.*

*14. Listene*r feels you understand them.

15. Leader's *communication* consists of three elements:

- Physical Appearance and Body Language – 55%
- Vocal Tone, Pace and Voice – 38%
- Verbal Communication – 7%

16. Lead employees to accomplish the *"community vision"* mission, goals of the organization.

Four Core Leadership Traits

Four Leadership Traits

1. Character Traits

- Integrity – Make the correct choice when faced with a right or wrong decision.

- Shows enthusiasm in attitude.

- Honesty

- Strong work ethic – Have a good work ethic

and take pride in working hard to achieve goals.

2. Leadership Analysis

- Uses good judgment
- Have a vision of what needs to be accomplished

3. Leadership Accomplishment

- Responsible for individual performance
- Responsible for group performance
- Driven to accomplish goals
- Takes initiative and does not wait to be told what to do

4. Interaction Leadership

- Excellent communication skills
- Relates well to others
- Inspires and motivates others
- Builds strong relationships

Leadership communication principles and traits will boost your confidence; provide skills to be an effective and successful leader at school, work, internships and in your community. These skills allow you to effectively market your achievements to a potential employer to get hired.

Chapter Seven
Problem Solving Interview Strategy

Problem, Action and Results (PAR'S)

Introduction

How do you solve problems?

In your career and life you will encounter problems you will need to solve. Learn how to solve problems by using strategies to empower you to accomplish your goals.

During an interview you may be asked a common interview question. "Tell me about a time you had a problem and what steps you took to solve it?"

The most effective way to present your problem solving skills is to review your accomplishments at school, volunteer work or another situation and create "short stories" of what your have done. In your short story describe the *problem, action* and *results.* When you speak each of these words the interviewer will easily be able to follow you and understand your problem solving skills.

Use the PAR formula to easily communicate how to define a problem, develop an action plan, and evaluate results.

The PAR Formula

Problem: Define the problem clearly. Set priorities and develop a strategy to address the problem.

Example: The **problem** I had was…

Action: Develop an action plan. Discuss the steps you used to achieve the plan.

Example: The **action** I took was…

Results: How well did you solve your problem? What did you learn that will be beneficial to solve or eliminate future problems?

Example: As a **result** of my action…

Prior to your interview write down and memorize three to six examples of PAR'S and practice them so you can confidently describe your problem-solving abilities.

Consider the following PAR actions steps when preparing for your interview.

Problem You Encountered

- What was the problem?
- Describe a non-routine challenging problem.

Action You Took To Solve the Problem

- How did you proceed?

- What specifically did you do?

- Present any creative or innovative skills.

- Describe what steps you took and how you did it.

- Describe challenges you faced and what you did to overcome them.

Results You Achieved

- What did you accomplish?
- Describe your achievements and contributions.

Listed is a **PAR** guide to help you complete the process.

Tell a "Short Story" of Your Knowledge, Skills and Abilities

Problem_____

Action_____

Results_____

Summary

What will problems solving skills do for me in my career?

Problem solving skills will increase your confidence and demonstrate your experience. When you identify a skill that is required for a position always provide an example by telling a "short story" of how you used your problem solving skills. The PAR strategy will give you the advantage over candidates who lack the skills to effectively describe how they solve problems.

The interviewer wants to see your skills in the position for which you have applied. The most effective way to communicate your skills and increase your chances of landing the job is to provide "examples" of your abilities.

Without providing examples you become just another candidate. The PAR Formula allows you the ability to "stand out" in an easy yet effective process and position you as a serious candidate of interest.

Ten Steps to Effective Time Management

Introduction

Do you manage time effectively? Do you need time management steps to walk you through the process?

Effective time management will enable you to plan and organize daily, weekly and monthly school, work or social events. The lack of planning will result in missed important dates and opportunities. Saying "I'm sorry, I forgot" in business is not acceptable or professional.

During an interview an employer may ask you "How do you manage your time at school or in your last job?"

Listed are steps you can use to improve time management and communicate to an employer how you achieve goals.

Ten Steps for Effective Time Management

Step 1: Identify Important Dates

- Use a calendar to plan for school, work, appointments, meetings, projects, activities and deadlines.

Step 2: Organize Goals by Priority

- Make a list of what needs to be done when and why.

- Make a list of what can be delegated to someone else.

Step 3: Delegation

- Who is the best person to complete the assignment?

- Understand you are ultimately responsible for the completion of the assignment.

- Follow-up with the delegated person in a timely manner to ask if they have questions and ensure the assignment is completed correctly and on time.

Step 4: Maximize your Time

- Maximize the time you have to complete your assignments and make it enjoyable.

Step 5: Be Realistic

- Set realistic time goals.

- Do not attempt to achieve more than you can manage.

- Allow for more time than is required so you will not be rushed.

Step 6: Focus

- Focus on one goal at a time.

Step 7: Plan for the Unexpected

- Make a plan for unexpected situations.

- Allow time for adjustments.

Always have a backup plan in mind.

Step 8: Motivate Yourself

- Stay positive.

- Motivate yourself to have a positive outcome.

Step 9: Learn when to say "No"

- Learn to say no to requests, activities or plans that are not the best use of your time.

Step 10: Plan Time for Personal and Social Activities

- Make a plan which includes time for personal and social activities.

Effective time management provides steps you can use to accomplish school, work, personal and social commitments. Although no plan is perfect use these guidelines and strategies to communicate how you plan and manage time.

Chapter Nine
Real Work Life Stress Management

Six Stress Management Strategies

Introduction

Do you get stressed out?

There are effective strategies to assist you in controlling stress at work, school and in your personal life. Being able to manage your frustrations and behavior will help you manage your emotions in a way that is positive and non-disruptive for others. Understand the triggers that create unhealthy responses and how to reduce stress when things are out of your control.

At an interview you may be asked "How do you manage stress?

You can answer the interviewer's question by discussing how you use the listed strategies to manage your stress.

Six Stress Management Strategies

Strategy 1: Acceptance

- Accept your present situation and use strategies to help you manage stress.

Strategy 2: Remove Yourself

- Remove yourself from the situation that causes stress.

- A time-out is a simple and effective stress management strategy.

- Take a walk or do some form of activity that will help you to relax without disturbing others.

Strategy 3: Relax

- Relax by choosing to write, read, sit silently or listening to music will help you to tune-out the situation and calm down.

Strategy 4: Recognize

- Recognize uncontrollable stress and identify the source it comes from.

- Work towards controlling behavior is the first step in managing confusion, emotions, envy, fear, frustration, sadness and others.

Strategy 5: Reflecting

- Reflecting on situations that caused you to react in a negative way will help you identify a solution to manage this behavior and avoid it in the future.

Strategy 6: Confront

- Before confronting a person – identify the root of the problem and the reason for the stress.

- Work towards calmly addressing the situation by using strategies that will help you go from stress to acceptance.

Four Unhealthy Anger Indicators

1. **Activities** – Spending too much personal time on the computer, watching too much television, substance abuse and others.

2. **Critical** – Very critical of others.

3. **Profanity** – Using profanity at school, work and personal situations.

4. **Lashing Out at Others** – Losing your temper and lashing out at others.

"Show you mean business."
                                        -PATRICIA DORCH

Chapter Ten
Interview Image

Suit Up for Success

Introduction

Do I need to wear a suit for an interview?

Planning your interview wardrobe is essential in conveying to the hiring manager you are serious about your career. Every employee should have a quality "interview suit" and shoes reserved in his or her wardrobe for interviews. A navy blue, black or dark gray makes a great first impression. Young ladies have a choice of wearing a pant or skirt suit to your interview. Add a blouse for ladies and a shirt and tie for young men to "show you mean business" in the eyes of the hiring committee.

What should I do if I do not have the recommended interview clothes and accessories?

Talk to your parents or guardian and ask for help in purchasing the clothes and accessories you need for your interview. There are interview image options you can use until you gain employment and purchase the recommended items at a later date.

During multiple interviews, be consistent in your professional appearance. Your attention to detail in your final interview is crucial to your success. Close the interview with your ability to perform the job. Once you are hired, project the same professional image you presented during your interview by dressing for success.

Young Men

Suit

- Solid color or small stripes
- Matching jacket and trousers
- Wear a long-sleeved shirt if you do not have a jacket
- Trousers cuffed or un-cuffed

Shirt

- Modified spread collar – non-button down collar – recommended
- Button down collar – optional
- White or light blue – no dark colors such as black or dark gray
- Long-sleeved – recommended
- Short sleeve – optional

Tie

- Solid, stripes or small patterns
- No red – red is the color of power

Shoes

- Lace-ups – recommended
- Slip-ons – loafer styles optional
- Dark color
- Polished and in good condition
- Sneakers – not recommended

Socks

- Dark color

- Match to trousers or shoes
- Mid-calf

Belt

- Match to trousers or shoes

Jewelry and Accessories

- Earrings – not recommended – do not wear during the interview process

- Bracelets – not recommended – do not wear during the interview process

- Tattoos – *Cover-up* during your interview with clothing or makeup

Hair

- Cut and styled
- Facial hair trimmed and groomed

Fragrance

- No cologne or scented aftershave

Nail Care

- Neatly trimmed

Attache Style Case (Optional)

- Leather

- Dark color – black or dark brown

- Stylish

- Not oversized

- No *backpacks* or *book bags*

Young Ladies

Suit

- Fashionable Style

- Solid Color or small stripes

- Pant or Skirt Suit

- No red or fashion colors

Dress

- Dress – optional
- Wear with a jacket or sweater look

Blouse

- Solid or small print or stripe
- No turtlenecks – wear if you have a visible tattoo on your neckline

Shoes

- Closed-toe – recommended
- A low heel is recommended over flat styles
- Dark color – Coordinate with suit
- Polished and in good condition
- Sandal styles – optional
- Flat shoe styles - optional

Jewelry and Accessories

- No ankle bracelets
- Tattoos – *Cover-up* during your interview with clothing or makeup

Hair

- Professionally styled
- No fashion hair colors such as red, blue, pink, purple etc.

Hose

- Coordinated with attire
- Bare legs – optional – not recommended

Makeup

- Conservative application
- Natural look - optional

Fragrance

- None

Nail Care

- Manicure or acrylic fills – no chipped nail polish
- No black, fashion bright colors or studs
- No long nails

Attache Style Case (Optional)

- Leather or soft style
- Dark color – preferably black or dark brown
- Stylish
- Not oversized
- No *backpacks* or *book bags*

Business Tools for Success
What You Should Bring To Your Interview
Young Men and Young Ladies

Business Tools for Success

- Leather writing tablet – dark color

- Quality ink pen with black ink

- Your personal business card

- Your personal name badge with your first and last name

Cell Phone

- Cell phone – TURN OFF!

Summary

A professional appearance is more important in business than ever before. Your appearance and body language always speak first. Appearances influence the opinions and perceptions others have of you.

Why do I need to dress up for an interview?

Dressing professionally for your interview shows respect for yourself, your career, and the organization to which you are seeking employment. To a great extent you are what you wear. Look confident and successful. Take the worry out of your interview image. Let it be your secret to success.

Show you mean business!

Chapter Eleven
Interview Etiquette

17 Rules for Interviewing

Introduction

Organizations commit a considerable amount of time and resources to interviewing and recruiting employees. They need to identify your *knowledge, skills,* and *abilities* in order to determine whether you are the best candidate for the job.

Your goal is to demonstrate how your knowledge and experiences can be of value to their organization. Use examples of past experiences, special assignments, internships, hobbies, volunteer work, and other activities to assist you in communicating your achievements.

At your interview your professional appearance is the first impression you make; your manners and professionalism become important afterwards. Learn the rules of interviewing to assist you in becoming more successful in achieving career goals.

17 Rules for Interviewing

Rule 1 – Appearance

- Wear a professional business suit with a matching top and bottom in the same fabric. Young ladies have the option of wearing a pant or skirt suit.

Rule 2 – Be On Time

- The interviewer interprets your arrival of fifteen to twenty minutes early, as your interest, commitment, dependability, and professionalism. Being late can show the opposite.

Rule 3 – First Impression

- Be kind to the receptionist. Do not smoke, use your cell phone, chew gum, eat anything or listen to a portable radio while you are waiting for your interview. You are being observed.

Rule 4 – Outer Coat

- Do not wear your outer coat into the interview. Take your coat off after you have spoken to the receptionist.

Rule 5 – Introductions

- If the interviewer uses both first and last name during introductions, use the last name when addressing him or her. For example: Ms. Jones or Mr. Jones. Introduce yourself by the name you *prefer* to be called.

Rule 6 – Handshake

- Give a confident handshake and smile when you shake hands. If you have sweaty palms dry them with a tissue prior to your introduction.

Rule 7 – Sitting Down

- Do not sit down until you have been invited to do so. *Ask* where they would like you to sit if there are multiple chairs.

Rule 8 – Preparing for the Interview

- What skills does the position require?

- What skills do you have that relate to the job description?

- What can you tell about your abilities that demonstrate your qualifications?

- Before the interview, think about two or three key skills you want the interviewer to know about you, and determine how to present them during the interview.

- Bring three copies of your resume, even though you know they already have a copy. Multiple resume copies prepare you for unexpected group interviews and show your professionalism.

- Review your resume prior to the interview. Be prepared to answer questions about your experience.

- Prepare and memorize five to seven questions you can ask about the position.

- Research the company and department of interest.

Rule 9 – Vocal Tone

- Match your vocal tone to the interviewer. Do not talk too loud or whisper when you speak.

Rule 10 – Body Language

Avoid signs of negative or power body language

- Slouching
- Avoiding Eye Contact
- Forced Smiles
- Swinging of Foot or Legs
- Crossing your Legs over your thigh – may be interpreted as a power statement
- Hand or Finger Movements

Rule 11 – Eye Contact

- Make eye contact, show self-confidence, and answer questions directly with a clear enthusiastic voice. Look directly at the interviewer when answering questions or asking a question.

Rule 12 – Be Positive

- Do not make any negative comments about your current status, teachers, co-workers, or former employers.

Rule 13 – Show You Want the Job

- Show initiative and give examples of your ability to perform the job.

Rule 14 – Close the Interview

- Close the interview by asking the interviewer if they have any concerns about your ability to perform the job.

- Overcome any objections to hiring you.

- Ask For The Job™.

- Wait for a response, thank the interviewer and ask about the next step in the interview process.

Rule 15 – Be Natural

- Be calm and natural during the interview closings.

Rule 16 – Thank you Letter

- After the interview email a formal thank you letter within 24 hours, however you should mail the hard copy.

- Thank each interviewer in a separate letter for taking time to meet with you. Make sure you have the correct spelling of their names and titles.

- In your thank you letter, identify two to four points your interviewer liked in *bullet format*. Use *spelling* and *grammar* check, and *re-read* your letter before mailing.

- Do not use your organizations in-house letterhead or mailing system if you are interviewing within your current organization.

Rule 17 – Follow-up

- Contact your interviewer within one week unless otherwise instructed as to your interview status.

Chapter Twelve
Cover Letter and Resume Writing

Introduction

What is the purpose of a cover letter?

The purpose of a cover letter is to summarize your experience and motivate an employer to invite you for an interview. The submission of your cover letter and resume is the first "written impression" of your skills. You only have a few minutes to showcase your communication skills and pass screening by human resources or talent management staff.

What is a Resume?

A resume is a *marketing* or *selling tool* which includes a written summary of your *knowledge, skills, abilities* and *accomplishments*. The purpose of the resume is to *"sell"* your achievements, create interest about your background and be invited for a face-to-face interview. The goal of a resume is how your knowledge, skills and abilities can add value to your employer – *not about what you want.*

Use the cover letter and resume as samples *only;* employers who receive templates of cover letters and resumes do not look at them favorably. Create your own business cover letter and resume design so you will uniquely stand out from other candidates.

The cover letter should include the position title, requisition number, location and other specific information listed on the job order. Listed are cover letter and resume tips and samples to assist you in the application process.

Nine Cover Letter Writing Tips

1. **Date** – Put the current date on your letter.

2. **Inside Address** – Put the company name and inside address if it is available.

3. **Title of Position** – Place below the company inside address.

4. **Requisition Number or Job Identification Number** – Place below the title of the position.

5. **Location –** Put the city and state below the requisition number.

6. **Create Letterhead** – Create your own letterhead with your contact information.

7. **Address Letter to** – Human Resources, Talent Acquisition Manager or a person's name that is listed on the job order. *Do not* use "To Whom It May Concern."

8. **Email Address** – Create a *professional* email address – No fun names.

9. **Personal Business Cards** – Purchase business cards or create them on your computer with a software program you can buy from a stationary store. Include your full name, address, professional email address, and telephone number.

Your Name

Your Street Address, City, State, Zip Code, and Telephone Number

Your Professional Email Address

SAMPLE

Cover Letter Etiquette

Today's Date

Company Name
Company Address (if provided)
City, State, Zip Code (if provided)

Position Title: Sales Associate – Look on the Job Order
Requisition Number or Job Identification Number: Look on the Job Order
Location: Look on the Job Order for City and State

Dear Human Resource Manager:

Thank you for the opportunity to present my skills for the (Name of Position) at (Name of Company).

My experience as a Sales Associate includes – Customer Service, Problem Solving, Interpersonal Communication, Business Etiquette and Follow-up skills.

Attached is my Resume and Cover Letter in a Word Document for your review.

Thank you for your time and consideration. I look forward to hearing from you.

Sincerely,

Sign your full name
Type your full name

Resume Writing Tips

Fifteen Resume Writing Tips

1. Resume Sections – Create common resume sections

   - Personal Information
   - Career Objective/Summary of Experience
   - Experience
   - Education
   - Activities and Accomplishments / Certificates and Awards

2. Keep it Simple – Keep your resume simple and easy to read.

3. Bullets – Use round bullets only.

4. Paragraphs – Do not write in paragraphs. Write sentences in *bullet* format.

5. Be Honest – Be honest about your background – sell yourself but do not over sell your skills.

6. Pictures and Artwork – Avoid pictures or artwork unless you are an actor, artist or model and your picture is requested by the employer.

7. References – Do not list personal or professional references on your resume. Create

a separate list of references and take it with you to your interview.

8. Fonts – Use a standard font such as Times Roman.

9. Resume Format – Save in a Word Document or PDF format.

10. Proofread for Spelling and Grammar – A word could be spelled correctly but used incorrectly on your resume.

11. Keywords – Use "keywords" that are used in your field and job description. Example – coordinated, planned, organized, inventoried or customer service.

12. Experience – List your employers, volunteer and internship information.

13. Accomplishments – List your key accomplishments for each employer in *bullet* format only.

14. Activities – List activities as it relates to the job description.

15. Paper – Use standard 8.5 by 11 quality white or cream color paper for your interview.

Your Name

Your Street Address, City, State, Zip Code, and Telephone Number
Your Professional Email Address

RESUME SAMPLE

Career Objective: To obtain a position in Retail that will lead to a Fashion Buyer where my creativity, organization, planning and follow-up skills will benefit my employer and increase sales.

EXPERIENCE

ABC Retail Store – City and State   Month/Year – Present or End Date
Sales Associate (Your Title)

- Coordinated the accurate count of markdowns and inventoried merchandise as scheduled.
- Performed daily assignments to ensure a neat, clean and organized store.
- Managed all customer services issues in a timely, friendly and professional manner.

EFG Retail Store – City and State   Month/Year – Month/Year
Sales Associate

- Maintained a clean work area at all times to promote products.
- Ensured proper merchandise presentation and operated the cash register as assigned.

EDUCATION

High School Diploma   Anticipated Date or Date Graduated
Name of School
City, State and Zip Code

ACTIVITIES / ACCOMPLISHMENTS

Name of Company – Volunteer – City and State   Month/Year – Month/Year
Name of School – Type of Award or Certificate   Month/Year

Chapter Thirteen
Top Interview Questions You May Be Asked

Introduction

Are you nervous about questions you may be asked at an interview? Are you prepared to answer interview questions you are asked? Are you unsure how to answer interview questions to get the job?

The ability to answer interview questions will enable you to confidently communicate your responses and advance to the next phase in the interview process. Listed are interview questions you may be asked and suggested ways to respond.

Sixteen Top Interview Questions and How to Respond

1. Tell me about yourself?

- "Yes, I would be happy to tell you about my experience, where would you like me to start?"

- When you ask an interviewer where they would like you to start, you will be able to focus *only* on the information they want to hear – not your life story.

2. What are your strengths?

- Talk about your strengths as it relates to the skills required in the job description.

3. What are your weaknesses?

- State a skill that is required for the job you do not have or needs improvement.

- Discuss your plans to learn or improve the skill.

- Do not state a weakness without a plan to improve it.

- Weaknesses should *not* be about anything personal.

4. How would you describe your proudest achievement?

- State an achievement such as an award, certificate, your role in a leadership program or class president and why you are proud of it. Keep your response short, powerful and to the point.

5. How do you plan your school or work day?

* Discuss how you use a planner for classes, projects, appointments, work assignments and other important dates.

* Discuss how you set priorities based on the importance of the assignment.

6. Do you have any questions?

* *Always* ask at least 3-5 questions.

7. What hourly wage or salary are you seeking for this position?

* *Always* ask what the hourly wage or salary *range* is *before* you state your desired income.

8. Describe your responsibilities in your last position.

* Talk about your *job description* and *accomplishments.*

9. What do you know about XYZ Company?

- Tell the interviewer you researched the company on the website.

- Talk about the company's mission, vision and goals.

- Talk about their products, services and customers.

10. What business tools do you use to keep yourself organized?

- Discuss how you use an electronic or paper planner.

- Discuss how you use a daily "to do list".

- Other business tools you use to be organized.

11. Why did you leave your last job or want to leave your current job?

- Do not say you want to leave a current position for more money although this could be one of your reasons. If your reason to leave is *only* for salary the employer will think you will leave their organization if you are offered a higher salary at another company.

- Explain you want to work for their organization to learn new skills, accept more responsibilities, make a contribution to their success, and for career advancement opportunities.

12. Why are you looking for employment?

- If this is your first job explain this information to the interviewer.

- Explain you want to work to learn new skills and help them accomplish their organization goals.

13. Tell me about a problem you had at school or work and the steps you took to solve it?

- Use the PAR Formula to discuss your problem solving process.

14. How do you manage your time?

- Discuss your time management strategies.

15. How well do you work with diverse groups of people?

- Provide an example how you interact with diverse groups of people at school, work, or other events.

16. Why should I hire you?

- Sell yourself.

- Talk about your top three strengths as it relates to the job and why you are the best and only candidate for the job.

Chapter Fourteen
Smart Interview Questions

Introduction

I nterview preparation starts with a candidate researching the organization and identifying the company mission, vision and goals, products and services.

Why do I need to ask interview questions?

Interview questions show your preparation, interest in their company and professionalism which is essential to moving forward in the interview process. Candidates who ask questions will be compared to those who do not. A lack of questions signals to the interviewer you have given little or no thought about the position.

What type of questions should I ask?

Ask questions that are important to your role and responsibilities that will help you make an employment decision. Often candidates are not called back for a second interview, because they have shown little or no interest in the position other than wanting or needing employment. Ask 3-5 questions at each interview. After the interview write down the responses the interviewer provided about your questions for future reference. Listed are suggested questions you can ask during the interview process.

Eleven Smart Interview Questions You Can Ask

1. Experience

- Where do you see my experience in this position?

2. Goals

- What goals can I help you accomplish for this position?

3. Management

- To whom would I report directly to for this position?

4. Leadership

- What type of leadership and personality are you looking for to fill this position?

5. Team Workers

- With whom will I work closely with for this position?

6. Projects

- Will I work on projects by myself or with others?

7. Work Schedule

- Which days of the week will I work and at what time? Does the work schedule change weekly or monthly?

8. Target Date

- What is your target date to fill this position?

9. Questions or Concerns

- Do you have any questions or concerns about my experience that I can clarify for you?

10. Close the Interview – Ask For The Job™

- I'm excited about the (Name of Position) and the opportunity to work for you and XZY Company - *"May I please have the job?"* Or, *"May I please have this career opportunity?"*

- Once you ask for the job – remain silent until the interviewer responds.

11. Close – The Next Step

- What is the next step in the interview process?

- Will I have another opportunity to discuss my experience in more detail?

Chapter Fifteen
Ask For The Job™

A Unique Interview Closing Strategy to Get Hired

Introduction

The most important step in the interview is the closing process. Your goal is to leave the interviewer with the impression you are the best candidate for the job.

Have you ever asked for a job?

Most job candidates do not "Ask For The Job™" which signals to the hiring manager you are not sure you want the job or uncomfortable asking for what you want. Asking for the job is a unique interview *closing* strategy that shows your interest and ability to *sell* yourself and close the interview with a possible job offer.

Never leave an interview without "*asking for the job*" and finding out what the next step in the interview process. When you ask – only what the next step is – it will provide a formality of steps – *not* the job offer. Listed are closing rules to consider when you interview.

Nine Interview Closing Rules

Rule 1: Ask Questions

* Ask questions about the company, job and management.

Rule 2: Reinforce your Accomplishments

* Reinforce your accomplishments by providing examples.

* Without examples you are just another candidate.

Rule 3: Address Interviewers Questions

* Address and overcome concerns or weaknesses the interviewer has about your ability to perform the job.

- Overcome objections by giving examples of your strengths in a specific area.

- If your interviewer has identified a weakness which is important for the job, state a plan of action to improve your skills.

- Once you state your strategy to overcome concerns you gain the support of the hiring manager. For example, if your weakness is organizational skills, you might say you use a planner to identify important dates and projects or you create a daily "to do list" and plan ahead to ensure projects and reports are completed on time.

Rule 4: Express Enthusiasm

- Express your *enthusiasm* for the position and company.

Rule 5: Ask For The Job™ - A Unique Interview Closing Strategy to Get Hired

- Ask for the job each time you are interviewed whether it is by an individual or panel.

- Always close – never leave assumptions you want the job.

- Never stop closing until you gain a job offer.

- Close the interview by "asking for the job."

How do I ask for the job - I've never done this before?

To get hired simply ask the hiring manager *"May I please have this career opportunity?"* or *"I'm excited about what we discussed today and the opportunity to work with you and XYZ Company, may I please have the job?*

- How you ask for the job will determine how the interviewer will respond. It's not what you say; it's how you say it that matters. Once you ask for the job wait patiently for the interviewer to respond.

- When you speak with confidence and sincerity in your voice you will be one step closer to gaining the job offer.

Rule 6: The Next Step

- Ask about the next step in the interview process so you will know what to expect for a second interview.

- Establish a time frame you can expect to hear from the interviewer or when you can follow-up on your interview status.

Rule 7: Thank the Interviewer

- Thank the interviewer for the time they have spent with you.

- Give a firm handshake, smile and make confident eye contact with the interviewer.

- Ask for the interviewer's business card so you can email a formal thank-you letter.

Rule 8: Thank-You Letter

- Send an email thank-you letter to your interviewers and reinforce your strengths.

- A thank-you letter is recommended over a thank you note – it allows you to continue to "sell" your skills to a potential employer.

- A thank-you note does not allow adequate space for you to reinforce skills discussed during your interview.

Rule 9: Follow-up

- Follow-up to determine the results of your interview.

Chapter Sixteen
Salary Negotiation

How to Ask for Your Desired Salary

Introduction

Are you comfortable asking for the salary you want?

Salary usually does not come up in the first interview, if it does and you are asked about your salary expectations it's recommended you *not* state an amount rather ask about the *salary range*. When you ask about the salary range you prevent yourself from possibly losing income as illustrated below.

How to Ask for Your Desired Salary

Candidate 1:

Hiring Manager: What salary are you expecting for Sales Associate position?

Candidate: I would like a salary of $8.00 per hour.

Hiring Manager: Great that sounds good.

Candidate 2:

Hiring Manager: What salary are you expecting for the Sales Associate position?

Candidate: Can you tell me what the salary range is for this position?

Hiring Manager: Yes, the hourly salary range is $8.00 - $12.00 per hour.

Candidate: Based on my skills and experience I believe $12.00 per hour is appropriate.

Although your salary might not start at $12.00 per hour, starting at the high range increases your chances of negotiating a desired salary based on your ability to perform the job. When you start at the low end of the range $8.00 it's difficult to increase what you initially stated you wanted. Candidate 1 possibly has lost $4.00 per hour. If you get into the habit of not asking for the salary range before you state an amount during your career it could add up to be a substantial amount of lost income.

If you are *offered* a salary of $8.00 per hour politely ask the hiring manager, is there a salary range for this position? Once you know what the range is you can ask for more money based on your experience.

If all new hires start at a specific amount per hour then you will receive the maximum salary. *Never assume the amount offered to you is the only salary.* The goal of the hiring manager is to hire the most qualified candidate and if possible save the company money.

Use this important and powerful negotiation strategy throughout your career to get your desired income. *Always ask questions before you state a salary and then negotiate for an agreed upon amount.*

Nine Secrets for New Hires

Introduction

Are you nervous about starting a new job?

Starting a new job is one of the most stressful experiences people face. The first 30, 60, or 90 day probationary period is crucial to your career success. Information you provide to your employer about your knowledge, abilities, integrity and communication skills will be put to the test. Before you speak, think about what you are going to say. Choose your words carefully, and be aware of your body language so that you are not misunderstood. Observe your environment while you are adjusting to your new role, responsibilities, people and the organizational culture.

Manage you internal social network by getting to know multiple people before you align yourself with any one person or group of people. People judge you by the company you keep. Take your time, be perceptive and use good judgment.

What should I do at new hire training?

During new hire orientation and training, be positive and upbeat; be a good listener and communicator. Get involved by participating – be a team player, and take a leadership role in training activities. Manage your attitude, behavior, and interactions with management and co-workers. Management will evaluate you based on your ability to perform your job and on your written, verbal, and non-verbal communication skills. At the end of your probationary period, they will determine if you are the right fit for the job and organization based on what they see and feedback from others.

Maintain a level of professionalism in new and future positions. Be dependable, approachable, and enthusiastic about a new career. Demonstrate your ability to manage multiple assignments and solve problems. Make a commitment to contribute to the success of organizational goals. Listed are secret strategies to help you be successful in your new job.

Nine Secrets for New Hires

Secret 1: Appearance: How Do I look?

Be consistent in your professional appearance throughout your career. Always be neat and clean.

- Clothing that is too short, tight, or revealing should not be worn to work.

- Uniforms or business casual clothing should be clean and pressed. Wash and wear clothing usually requires a light pressing.

- Self expression art, such as piercings and tattoos, are inappropriate for business and should not be visible. Remove them or cover them up with make-up or clothing.

- If you are unsure if you should wear or expose it, do not.

Secret 2: First Day at Work

- Arriving fifteen minutes early will make a good first impression.

- Be friendly, positive, and focused.

- Be prepared to complete new hire paperwork.

- Bring a pen with black ink and a writing tablet.

Secret 3: New Hire Orientation

- Introduce yourself to management and others.

- Be open to changes and new challenges.

- Be aware of your tone when you speak.

- Bring personal information you need for identification such as your driver's license, social security card and other required documents.

Secret 4: New Hire Training

- Always be on time.

- Conduct yourself as a young professional.

- Do not fall asleep in training.

- Participate and volunteer for training activities.

Secret 5: Employment Expectations

- Ask for a copy of your job description if you do not have one.

- Ask questions about your role, responsibilities, and expectations of your performance.

- If you are sick, will be late for work, or have a personal emergency, contact your immediate supervisor and advise them of your situation. Leave a voice mail message *and* an e-mail message specifying your situation and the time you plan to arrive to work.

Secret 6: Understand What is Expected of You

Take time to understand what is expected of you in existing and future career roles. Review you job description with your supervisor, and identify new skills you can learn and others you can improve upon to successfully complete your probationary period. The knowledge and skills you learn will position your for your *next* job.

How often should I talk to my supervisor about my performance during the probationary period?

It's essential to take the initiative to meet with your supervisor in 30, 60, and 90 days to gain valuable feedback about your performance. Ask what skills can be improved and what steps are necessary to accomplish the skills they have identified. Let your supervisor be your "champion" for your career development – never forget that it's ultimately up to you to manage your own career. Listen and be open to critique that will enable you to improve and acquire new skills. Use resources available to achieve department goals and increase your visibility in the organization.

Knowledge, Skills and Abilities (KSAs)

- What skills will I need for career development?
- What abilities do I have that require improvement?
- *Always* make your manager look good.
- Have one-on-one meetings with your manager on a regular basis.
- Contribute to your department goals.
- Learn new skills for promotional opportunities.

Secret 7: Workplace Profanity

There are *no* excuses or exceptions for using profanity or words that translates to curse words. The use of the word *"freakin"* or other slang words shows your lack of maturity, character, intelligence, emotional control and professionalism.

Secret 8: Employee Internet Search

If a new or potential employer did an Internet search on you, what would they find out about you?

- Do not allow your past or future behavior to sabotage your career.

- Think twice before your participate in social activities that might appear on social networking sites where your behavior may be inappropriate.

- Information on the internet is difficult to remove. Be prepared to explain comments and pictures that are unfavorable about your character.

- You could risk losing your job or a career opportunity if your employer has concerns about your perception to management, co-workers and customers.

Secret 9: Company Surveillance: Do You Know Who is Watching You?

More than eighty percent of companies monitor their employees' communications. You have no privacy at work. Be selective with your choice of words in written communication to others. Do not think your personal e-mails to co-workers, family, and friends are none of your employer's business during and after business hours. Keep in mind the computer is the property of your employer.

Employers might observe you using any of the following resources:

- Blog surfing
- Web traffic
- Computer files
- Instant Messaging
- Interior and exterior cameras, visible and invisible to you
- Phone calls
- E-mails
- Satellite tracking for a company cell phone, computer and car
- Text messages

"Social success begins with you."
-PATRICIA DORCH

Chapter Eighteen
Dining Etiquette

The Taste of Career Success

Introduction

Everyday a business meal is used for an interview, breakfast, lunch, teatime, and dinner. Professionals use business meals for performance reviews, promotions, meetings, conferences, meeting clients, presenting products and services, networking and other reasons.

Why are table manners important?

Table manners play an important role in making a positive impression. Visible signs of your manners are essential to your professional success. Your social skills are on display; never assume others will not notice or be understanding of poor table manners. Polished table manners speak volumes about your professionalism and can help advance your career.

Business Dining Etiquette

Napkin Use

- Place your unfolded napkin on your lap.

- The napkin remains on your lap during the entire meal.

- Use your napkin to gently blot your mouth during your meal.

- At the end of the meal, place your napkin on the right of your dinner plate.

- Do not refold or bundle up your napkin.

Ordering

- Ask your server questions you might have about the menu.

- As a guest, do not order one of the most expensive items on the menu.

- Young ladies orders are usually taken before young men's.

- Your server will determine how to take your order.

The Pre-Set Table Setting

As a general rule, liquids are on your right side and solids are on your left.

To The Right

- Glassware
- Cup and saucer
- Knives and spoons
- Seafood fork, if seafood is included in the meal

To The Left

- Bread and butter plate
- Small butter knife is placed horizontally across the top of the plate
- Salad plate
- Napkin and forks

Use of Silverware

- The rule of silverware usage is work your silverware from the outside in.

- Use one utensil for each course.

- The salad fork is on the outer left, followed by your dinner fork.

- Your soup soon is on your outer right, followed by your dinner knife.

- Dessert spoon and fork are placed above your plate or brought out with the dessert.

American vs. European Style

American Style

- Cut food by holding your knife in the right hand and the fork in the left hand.

- Change your fork from your left hand to your right hand to eat, with the fork tines facing down.

- If you are left-handed, keep your fork in your left hand, tines facing up.

European (or Continental) Style

- Cut food by holding your knife in your right hand while securing your food with your fork in your left hand.

- Your fork remains in your left hand, tines facing down.

- Your knife is in your right hand.

- Eat small pieces of food.

- Pick food up with your fork, which is in your left hand.

When You Have Finished Your Meal

- Do not push your plate away from you.

- Lay your fork and knife diagonally across your plate.

- Place your knife and fork side by side with the sharp side of the blade facing inward. The fork tines should face down. The knife and fork should be positioned at 10 and 4 o'clock.

- Do not place used silverware back on the table. Place it on the saucer. Unused silverware should be left on the table.

- Leave a soup spoon on your soup plate.

Business Table Manners

- **Doggy bag**: Do not ask for a doggy bag if you are a guest. Reserve doggy bags for informal dining.

- **Finger foods**: Finger foods can be messy and are best left for informal dining. Order foods that can be eaten with a knife and fork.

- **Smoking**: Do not smoke while dining out; this might offend your guest. People form opinions of you based on what they see and smell.

- **Body language**: Do not slouch; sit up straight at the table.

- **Resting your hands**: When you are not eating, keep your hands in your lap or resting on the table, with your wrists on the edge of the table. Elbows on the table are acceptable between courses but not during meals.

- **Food Seasoning**: Do not season your food before you have tasted it.

- **Chewing**: Never chew with your mouth open or make noises when you eat. Do not talk with your mouth full.

- **Slurping your soup:** Do not slurp your soup

from the spoon or pick the bowl up to your mouth. Spoon your soup away from you when you take it out of the bowl. Do not blow your soup if it is hot; wait for it to cool.

- **Food between your teeth**: If you cannot remove the food between your teeth with your tongue, excuse yourself from the table and go to the rest room where you can remove the food in private. Those foods might include broccoli, spinach, fresh ground pepper, seeds, cereals or corn on the cob.

- **Eating bread and rolls**: Tear and butter one piece at a time.

- **Conversation**: Engage in lively conversation free of controversial topics such as politics, race, religion, or sex.

- **Leaving the table**: If you leave the table during the meal, simply excuse yourself.

- **Out of your reach**: If you need something on the table that is out of your reach, politely ask the person closest to the item to pass it to you.

- **Fallen silverware**: If a piece of silverware falls on the floor pick it up if you can reach it. Politely ask the server to bring you a replacement.

- **Food and liquid spills**: If food spills off your plate, pick it up with a piece of your silverware and place it on the edge of your plate. If a liquid spills, clean it up as much as you can, and limit the attention you draw to yourself.

- **Bad food**: Never spit out a piece of bad food or gristle into your napkin. Discreetly remove the food from your mouth with your utensil and place it on the edge of your plate. You may choose to cover it up with other food on your plate.

- **Dry mouth**: Keep your mouth moist. A dry mouth can cause white saliva deposits to appear on your lips, and in the corners of your mouth without your knowledge.

Chapter Nineteen
Thank You Etiquette

Introduction

Did you remember to say thank you?

There are many people with whom you interact daily. Saying "thank you" is important and effective in building relationships in interviews, with your classmates, co-workers, managers and customers. Thanking others makes a positive reflection on you and the business organization's ability to succeed and achieve goals. A thank you card can be displayed on a desk as a reminder of your appreciation an admired by others. A thank you card shows your professionalism and makes you stand out from others. There are many reasons and situations you may choose to say thank you listed are a few suggestions.

In business it's the little things that count, and pay off in a big way.

Co-workers

• Co-workers usually provide assistance when working together on projects and other daily tasks.

Managers and Supervisors

- Managers and supervisors provide support, feedback and leadership for your career.

Gifts

- Be gracious when receiving gifts, even if you do not like what you receive.

- Always check with your company's "Code of Conduct" policy before you accept gifts from customers.

Thank-you customs

- Thank you gifts and customs vary based on culture.

Written Thank-You Notes

- Written thank-you notes are more personal and convey special appreciation.

- Short two-or-three line messages are sufficient.

- Timely thank-you notes are sincere and easier

to write when done within one week.

- Make a specific reference to the gift or reason for your thank you.

- Thank-you notes are for "thank-yous," not for business discussions.

Thank You Emails

- An email thank you is appropriate when conducting everyday business.

Chapter Twenty
Career Fairs

Making Connections Face to Face

Introduction

Do you attend career fairs?

Career and job fairs are essential in your job-search strategy and one of the most effective ways to get hired. You have the opportunity to market your skills to dozens of employers at one location.

In a fair–like atmosphere it's important you take the event seriously and make a positive first impression just as you would in an employer's office. *Do not underestimate the importance of your business image, behavior, body language, manners and overall professionalism.*

Employers attend career fairs to find qualified candidates who have a positive attitude, are prepared, shows initiative and a sincere interest in working for their organization. Be ready to promote yourself and sell your skills on the spot.

Tell employers about your experiences and why you are the best candidate for the job.

Research your targeted companies that will be attending the career fair to identify which positions would be a match for your skills and experience. Make a primary and secondary target list of employers and spend *quality time* specifically marketing your skills to those employers. Knowing what you want shows you have done your home work. Collect business cards from employer representatives with whom you discuss career opportunities. Within 24 hours send a formal email thank-you letter to each of your contacts.

There will be other job seekers marketing their skills – leave a favorable and lasting impression in the minds of employers you meet. Be kind and engaging and make the most of your time at each employer booth.

Preparing For a Career Fair

A career fair event is the place to show you are serious and interested in gaining employment with a potential employer. These guidelines will prepare you with strategies and tips to manage a career fair. Job seekers who are most successful at career fairs are those who prepare. Before attending a career fair, it's essential to know to how to plan, execute and follow-up after the career fair.

Three Smart Preparation Strategies

1. **Plan y**our career fair strategy
2. **Execute** your career fair strategy
3. **Follow-up** after your career fair

Plan Your Career Fair Strategy

Business Image

Can I wear jeans to a career fair?

Your face-to-face contact with a potential employer is your "first interview" whether you have an appointment or not. Casual attire is *inappropriate* and communicates you are not serious about your career. The fact that you will only spend a few minutes at each employer's booth does not lessen the importance of your image.

Many employers have criteria they use when they meet you and image is at the top of the list. Employers may note on your resume or application your "first impression" did not meet their expectations. If you ever wondered why you were not contacted after an interview perhaps your image excluded you from the hiring process.

- Plan to wear a "business suit" to make a positive first impression.

- Do not wear casual attire to the career fair – this could be a career limiting move.

- Your accessories, personal grooming and cleanliness should be impressive.

- Do not wear perfume or cologne.

- Make sure your teeth are clean with fresh breath.

Resume

- Always bring adequate copies of your resume printed on resume paper to work the career fair.

- Proofread your resume so there are no errors.

Reference List

- Have a list of your professional references prepared as part of your career portfolio.

- Provide contact information such as; contact name, title, company name, address, direct telephone number or extension, email address and if your reference is professional or personal contact. Indicate if your reference prefers phone or email contact. An example has been prepared for you.

Reference Contact Information

Company Name
Contact Name
Contact Title
1234 Career Way
Career, CA 12345
Email address *(Preferred)*
Telephone Number
Cell Phone *(Optional)*
(Professional Reference)

Written References

- Include written references from employment, internships or volunteer work in your portfolio.

- References written on company letterhead are most impressive.

Research

- Research companies you have an interview appointment with and those on your target list.

Prepare your 30-Second Commercial or Interview Sales Pitch

- Prepare and practice your 30 second commercial to promote and sell yourself.

Writing Tablet, Pen and Calendar

- Take a writing tablet of white paper in a leather portfolio to take notes after the interview or write down follow-up information.

- Use a quality name brand ink-pen with black ink for business.

- Do not use a pencil – it is a casual accessory and takes away from your business image.

- Take your personal calendar and be prepared to schedule a second interview on the spot.

Prepare Questions

- Be prepared with intelligent uncommon questions to ask the interviewer.

- Practice out loud your responses to interview questions you might be asked.

- Do not ask questions you could obtain answers to by going to the company website.

Location

- Know the exact location of the career fair and the parking situation including parking fees.

Be On Time

- If you have a scheduled interview be on time and arrive 20 minutes prior to your interview time.

Program Floor Plan

- Study the floor plan so you will know where your interview or company targets are located.

Execute Your Career Fair Strategy

Resume Presentation

- Carry copies of your resume and references in a professional portfolio.

- Volunteer your resume – do not wait for the interviewer to ask for it.

Respect Everyone

- Treat every person you encounter with courtesy and respect. Employers do solicit input from other team members during hiring decisions.

Handshake

- Greet your interviewer with a confident handshake and sincere smile.

Listen

- Listen to the correct pronunciation of your interviewer's name and title.

- Listen to information about positions that might be of interest to you.

Title

- Address your interviewer by title (Ms, Mr., and Dr.) and last name unless invited differently.

Business Card

- Ask your contacts for their business cards.

- Use the contact information to email a thank-you letter and mail the original copy after the event.

Eye Contact

- Maintain good eye contact during your interview.

Sitting

- Take a seat only if you are invited to do so.

- Be still in your seat and avoid crossing your leg over your thigh. Crossing your leg over your thigh is considered "power" body language.

- Place your feet flat on the floor or cross them at your ankles to be more comfortable.

Interviewer Questions

- Respond to questions and provide examples of your achievements.

- A "short story" about your achievements helps the interviewer remember you and see you in the position.

Clarification

- Ask for clarification if you do not understand a question or procedure.

Thorough Responses

- Be honest, thorough and concise in your responses.

Be Yourself

- Do not "over-sell" your skills – you want a good career match between you and your employer.

Be Serious

- Treat the interview seriously and show the interviewer you are sincere about the career opportunity.

Be Positive

- Show a positive upbeat enthusiastic attitude.

Win-Win

- Evaluate the interviewer and organization. The goal is for a win-win outcome. Think about how you are treated and conduct yourself professionally.

Close – Ask For The Job™

- Practice "asking for the job"- in your own environment so you will feel confident and comfortable expressing what you want – the job offer.

- If you are seriously interested in the career opportunity close – Ask For The Job™.

- You can do this by simply and confidently – not being arrogant use one of these closing strategies – *"May I please have this career opportunity?"* or *"May I please have the job?"* or *"May I please move to the next step in the interview process?"*

- It's not what you say when you ask for the job, it's *how you say it* that counts.

- Once you ask for the job – remain silent until the interviewer responds.

- The goal in "closing" the interview is to ask for what you want – the job offer.

- Asking an employer for the job is *"promoting"* or *"selling"* you. This unique strategy can position you for a second interview and a job offer.

Interview Process

- Ask the employer about the interview process, when and from whom you can expect to hear from them.

- Identify what action you are expected to take in the interview process.

Interview Close

- When the interviewer closes the interview, give a firm handshake, make positive eye contact and smile.

- Thank the interviewer for their time and company materials they have given you.

During the Career Fair – Interview Don'ts

Attitude

- Don't exhibit a negative attitude during an interview. Stay positive and the job search process will have its rewards.

Body Language

- Don't slouch, sit on the edge of your chair or act anxious. Be aware and in control of your non-verbal body language.

Cell Phone

- Turn It Off!

- Don't take your cell phone with you during an interview if you travel by vehicle – leave it in your car.

- Don't underestimate the power of your first impression if your cell phone goes off during an interview.

- Don't have a cell phone ear-piece in your ear.

- Don't take a cell phone call if you forget to turn off your phone; turn off your phone, apologize and continue with your interview.

- Don't use a cell phone while you are walking around to employer booths; you are being observed. If you need to use your cell phone, leave the room of the career fair event.

Children, Friends, Parents and Pets

- Don't take children, friends, parents or pets with you. An assistance animal is not considered a pet.

Desperate

- Don't appear to be desperate for employment; don't appear to take any job offered.

False Information

- Don't falsify information on your application documents or interview questions.

Gum, Mints or Smell like Smoke

- Don't chew gum or suck mints.

- Don't smell like smoke. Smelling like smoke will be a turn-off to a new employer – especially one who does not smoke.

- Don't have anything in your mouth including a ring piercing.

Interviewer's Questions

- Don't be unprepared for common interview questions about your background. A lack of preparation could eliminate you from the selection process.

Know What You Want

- Don't expect the interviewer to know what type of work you are interested in; do your research to identify the best position for your skills and experience.

Negative Comments

- Don't make negative comments or remarks about teachers, previous employers, internships or volunteer work whether you were paid or not.

Practice

- Don't use the interview as practice for another position.

- Don't treat your interview opportunity casually.

Salary

- Don't ask questions about or give the impression you are only interested in salary.

- Don't ask about company benefits or other perks until the subject is discussed with you by your interviewer.

Follow-up after the Career Fair

Take Notes

- After each interview with an employer, take notes so you will not forget key points mentioned during your meeting.

- Do not take notes during your interview unless you ask for permission to write down follow-up information.

- Do not take notes during the entire interview.

Thank-You Letter

- Type your thank-you letter and email it within 24 hours.

- A thank-you letter should restate key skills in bullet format they liked about your background.

Follow-up

- Follow-up when you are instructed to do so.

- Lack of follow-up skills can be the difference between achieving the next step in the interview process or a missed career opportunity.

Ten Career Fair Quick Tips

Career fairs are excellent places to meet with employers, attend seminars, network and land a new career. Make the most of your time marketing your skills and selling yourself to employers so you will achieve your career goals.

1. Prepare to Interview

    - Be prepared to interview on the spot.

    - Quickly and effectively sell your skills, talents, experiences and yourself.

    - Have a salary figure in mind in case the topic comes up. Always ask what the salary range is *before* you state your requirements.

2. Research

- Visit targeted employer's websites.

- Read business articles and other valuable information so you will "stand out" from other candidates.

3. Resumes

- Take multiple copies of your resume on quality paper.

- Organize your personal information in a brief case or portfolio *not* a *backpack* or *book bag*.

4. Job Application

- Be prepared to neatly fill out an application on the spot in *black* ink.

- Take your employment, internships and volunteer work history dates and reference information with you.

- Avoid taking your application home to complete it. This allows your competition to gain the advantage.

5. Arrive Early

- Arrive 20 minutes early if you have a scheduled interview appointment.

- Arrive 30 minutes early to register and plan your career fair strategy.

- Review an employer booth floor plan if one is available.

6. Targeted Employers

- Visit your targeted employers first.

- Market your skills to other employers.

7. Collect Business Cards

- Collect business cards from each employer you meet.

- Email a thank-you letter to your contacts within 24 hours.

8. Take Notes

- Take notes after you speak with each employer while the information is fresh in your mind.

9. Closing the Interview

- When closing the interview ask the employer what is the next step in the interview process.

- If an employer informs you they will contact

you – ask for permission to contact them if you have not heard from them within a specific time.

10. Visit Websites of Targeted Employers

- Visit websites of targeted employers that are of interest to you.

- Post your resume and complete an application online if you have not done so.

Seven Career Fair Bonus Tips

1. Personal Business Card

- Take your personal business cards with you for networking.

- Have a professional email address and your contact information.

2. Job Search Seminars

- Attend job search seminars after you have met with your targeted employers.

3. Networking

- Attend networking gatherings to be visible and meet new contacts.

4. Interviewers Time

- Don't monopolize the interviewer's time. Be sensitive to others standing in line behind you.

5. Stand Alone

- Do stand alone and be independent of others.
- Be aware some employer's interview in groups.

6. Negative Words

- Avoid negative words like – "I can't", "I'm not", or "I won't".

7. Conversation Etiquette

- Don't invite yourself into a conversation an interviewer is having with another job seeker. Patiently wait for your turn to speak.

Summary

During your meetings with employers provide examples of your experience and skills. Career fairs provide a valuable resource and benefits for you to explore careers and seek employment options. Career fairs enable you to:

- Market your skills to multiple industries.

- Gain valuable interview experience and advice from industry experts.

- Find out about key positions and submit your resume and application in person.

- Identify employment, internships, research experiences and volunteer opportunities.

- Develop a network of new contacts.

Know what skills you have to offer and show employers the one asset they can't do without is YOU!

Chapter Twenty One
How to Resign Gracefully

Career Exit Strategy

Introduction

If you determine before or at the end of your probationary period that you are not a good match for the position and no longer want to work for the organization, listed are guidelines to assist you. These guidelines also apply if you have accepted a career opportunity with another organization.

Volunteer Resignation – Do:

- Type a dated letter of resignation and present it to your manager or supervisor before you discuss it with your co-workers.

- Keep a copy of your resignation letter for your files.

- Give two weeks notice, and state your last day in the letter. Do not put your new employers name in your letter.

- Be prepared for the employer to ask you to leave immediately if this is during your probationary period or if you have accepted a job offer with a competitor.

- Ask what you can do to make your transition a smooth one.

- Wish your manager good luck in his or her career.

- Thank your manager for the career opportunity.

Do Not:

- Email or text message your resignation.

- Walk out without giving notice.

- Brag about where you are going.

- Tell other people why you are leaving.

- Show up late, not show up at all, or call in sick after you have given notice unless you absolutely have to.

- Bad mouth your employer to your next career opportunity or on social networking sites.

Termination

If you are terminated during or at the end of your probationary period or at some point in your career, the following guidelines may assist you.

*   Ask why you are being terminated if you do not know.

*   Accept the termination.

*   Do not argue.

*   Do not cry.

*   Do not beg for your job back.

*   Do not have a bad attitude, use profanity, throw things, or threaten anyone.

*   Ask for a "Letter of Reference" on company letterhead if you have been downsized or have another career opportunity.

Whether you leave on your own terms, are terminated, or your position is eliminated, demonstrate the same professional behavior and attitude you used to get hired. Leave with grace and class on a positive note. You never know when people you have worked with in the past may be in a position to hire or promote you in a future career opportunity.

Job Search
Teen Interview Tips and Strategies to Get Hired

Summary

Are you looking for a job? Are you faced with lots of competition? Do you need more skills to compete for a good job? Developing new skills takes initiative, time, self-confidence, practice, commitment and action.

Job Search: Teen Interview Tips and Strategies to Get Hired is a comprehensive career guide to gain employment. Job Search provides interview, interview image, communication, business and social etiquette, and professionalism skills to enable you to stand out and compete in the workplace.

In a competitive business environment few people will share with you the secrets in this book to improve your skills. Take ownership and the initiative to learn new skills and apply your knowledge to achieve your career goals.

Book Review:

You are invited to write a book review at:

www.amazon.com and www.barnesandnoble.com

Success Story or Interview Questions:

Do you have a success story or interview question?

Please send me an email to share your success stories or interview questions.

PatriciaDorch@jobsearchteensbook.com

Patricia@execudress.com

Thank you for sharing your feedback.

ABOUT THE AUTHOR

PATRICIA DORCH is President and CEO of EXECU DRESS. She has a Master of Science in Business Organizational Management from the University of LaVerne in LaVerne, California. Patricia has a background in Sales and Marketing for major medical, healthcare and business corporations.

Patricia is the author of *Professionalism: New Rules for Workplace Career Success, Job Search: New Get Hired Ideas, Tips and Strategies for 40 Plus and Six Figure Career Coaching Advice: The Ultimate Guide To Achieving Success.* Patricia is an in-demand career expert who specializes in maximizing the potential for professionals to get hired, demonstrate professionalism in the workplace and get promoted in today's ultra competitive job market. Patricia has an extraordinary ability to see career opportunities hidden in plain view. Patricia Dorch's message is clear – "Take responsibility for your career and brand your professional brilliance for unparallel success."

Speaker Services:

Are you looking for a speaker? Would you like to add meet the Author and Book signing to your teen program?

Patricia is a dynamic speaker, trainer and consultant – schedule her for your next teen conference, career day, graduation or leadership program, interview skills seminar, meeting, local, regional or national event at:

Website: www.jobsearchteensbook.com
Email: PatriciaDorch@jobsearchteensbook.com

Website: www.execudress.com
Email: Patricia@execudress.com

JOB SEARCH

TEEN
INTERVIEW TIPS AND STRATEGIES TO
GET HIRED

PATRICIA DORCH

CPSIA information can be obtained at www.ICGtesting.com
Printed in the USA
LVOW011322180413

329824LV00004B/17/P